Brother

Yun

The Heavenly Man
of China

Rebecca Davis

Potter's Wheel Books

Pennycress Publishing
Greenville, South Carolina

Brother Yun: the heavenly man of China / Rebecca Davis.

Summary: A biography for children of one of the leaders of the under-ground church in Asia's largest nation.

Christian biography
Liu Zhenying (Brother Yun), 1958-.
Juvenile nonfiction / Biography and autobiography / Religious
ages 7-10

Cover design by Tim Davis
Photo credit Chinese New Testament: Dunham Bible Museum, Houston Baptist University, used by permission.

Pennycress Publishing
Greenville, SC 29609
ISBN: 9780998943503

The Lord is my light and my salvation;
Whom shall I fear?
The Lord is the strength of my life;
Of whom shall I be afraid?
When the wicked came against me
To eat up my flesh,
My enemies and foes,
They stumbled and fell.
Though an army may encamp against me,
My heart shall not fear;
Though war may rise against me,
In this I will be confident.

Psalm 27:1-3

Books by Rebecca Davis

Potter's Wheel Books
Showing children the Master Potter at work
—

#1 Fanny Crosby: Queen of Gospel Songs
#2 Joy Ridderhof: Voice Catcher Around the World
#3 George Mueller: Pickpocket to Praying Provider
#4 Brother Yun: The Heavenly Man of China

ଚଠଔଃ

With Daring Faith: A Biography of Amy Carmichael

ଚଠଔଃ

the Hidden Heroes series
True Stories of God at Work Around the World
(Christian Focus Publications)

#1 With Two Hands
Stories of God at Work in Ethiopia

...

#2 The Good News Must Go Out
Stories of God at Work in the Central African Republic

...

#3 Witness Men
True Stories of God at Work in Papua, Indonesia

...

#4 Return of the White Book
True Stories of God at Work in Southeast Asia

...

#5 Lights in a Dark Place
True Stories of God at Work in Colombia

...

#6 Living Water in the Desert
True Stories of God at Work in Iran

...

For more information visit *www.hiddenheroesmissionarystories.com*

Contents

Chapter 1

How Did Father Get Well?

Yun lay on his mat, tossing and turning. How would his family survive if Father died? They had already spent all their money trying to find a way to cure his cancer. They'd even sold everything they could. Then Father had called for a priest to cast the demons of sickness out of him. But he only got worse.

The situation seemed very bleak. The family worked in the field, but that didn't give them enough food. Even now they had to beg from their neighbors. After Father died, would they starve?

The skinny teenager tossed and turned on his mat.

Suddenly Yun felt a hand shaking his shoulder. "My son, wake up!" His mother's urgent voice called him.

"I'm awake. What's wrong? Is Father . . . gone?"

"No! Come in here. Come, all of you." Mother motioned to the other children. "I have something to tell you."

They all gathered around Mother. "I heard a voice," she explained intensely. "Clear and tender and full of love." She clasped her hands and lifted her eyes to the sky. "The voice said 'Jesus loves you.'"

"Who is Jesus?" asked Yun.

"He is the only hope for Father," Mother replied. "Long ago, thirty years ago, I gave my life to Him. But then the Communists came. . . ." Suddenly she covered her face with her hands. "All religion was destroyed. Many Christians were killed. I didn't know much about Jesus, and I forsook Him. But then tonight I heard His voice! Tonight I gave my life back to Him!"

Yun and the others gazed at her, amazed.

"Jesus is the only hope for Father," Mother repeated. "We must cry out to Him for Father's healing."

Immediately all of them went to Father's bed. They gathered around him and cried, "Jesus, please heal Father! Jesus, heal Father!" Through the night, they continued to cry out to the God of heaven.

In the morning, Father looked at them all. "I'd like something to eat," he said. It was the first time he had wanted food in months!

Within a week Father was completely well. The cancer was gone, and he was whole and strong.

"We must tell all the people in our village!" Mother whispered. "We have to tell everyone!"

"We can't have a public gathering," said Yun. "Public gatherings are illegal."

Chapter 1

"But we can have a private gathering," said his mother.

"Those are illegal too," said Yun.

"But I have a plan. All of you go invite our friends and relatives to come to our house. Don't tell them why. They'll likely think they're coming to a funeral!" She laughed with delight.

Yun and his siblings went from house to house. They invited friends and relatives, but didn't tell why.

When they arrived back at their mud hut, the friends and relatives were in for a surprise. There was Father himself! He stood at the door of the house, healthy and whole.

"Come in, come in!" Mother whispered. She locked the door and covered the windows. "I want to tell you how my husband was made well."

Everyone was eager to listen.

"We prayed to Jesus," she said triumphantly. "Jesus!"

Some of the younger neighbors didn't know what she was talking about. But others gasped in shock. They knew it was definitely against the law to pray to Jesus. Some of them knew about Jesus from many years ago. That was before the Communists sent all the missionaries away. That was before so many Christians had been killed.

"Last week I heard His gentle voice!" Yun's mother continued. "He told me He loved me. Then He healed my husband. I gave my life to Him when I was young, but then . . . it became so hard." She covered her face with her hands again.

The older villagers murmured agreement. They knew about Christians who had been killed for their faith in Jesus Christ.

"But no more," Yun's mother said, wiping her tears. "I will not forsake Him again. I'll follow Him forever. He is a loving Master. He is the one who saves and heals!" Then Mother looked at all of them. She said, "You too! You must follow Him too! He is the one who saves and heals!"

Chapter 1

Every single one of those friends and relatives kneeled down on the floor. All of them cried out to Jesus to be their Master too.

Mother didn't have a Bible. Even if she did, she couldn't read. But she knew Jesus loved them and came to save them. She grew bolder and told others in the village, more and more and more. "Jesus healed my husband! He loves us! Follow Him!"

Chapter 2

If I Don't Get a Bible, I'll Die!

Yun often asked his mother the same question. "Mother, can you tell me more about Jesus?"

"He is the Son of the God of heaven," Mother answered. "He died on the cross for us, to take our sins and sicknesses."

"But I know that part already. Can you tell me anything else?" Yun was sixteen years old and very hungry to learn more about Jesus.

"I can't, my son. The words and deeds of Jesus were written in the Bible, but all the Bibles are gone." Yun's mother shook her head with great sadness.

"Where did they go?"

Mother set her lips tight and shook her head, looking at the ground. Then Yun understood. They had been destroyed by the leaders of the Chinese government.

"But our people had Bibles in the past, right? What does a Bible look like?"

"I don't know," Mother answered sadly. "I saw some holy words written on a paper once, but that wasn't a Bible. I met some people who said they had seen a Bible, but that was a long time ago."

"There must still be some Bibles in China," Yun muttered to himself. He began to go from house to house where he knew the Christians lived. "Have you ever seen a Bible?" he asked.

"I once saw a few bits of Scripture written out by hand," said one.

"I did too," said another.

Then in one house, one old person said, "I remember seeing a Bible when I was young."

"You did?" Yun asked eagerly. "What did it look like?"

"It was a book," she answered. "About this big, and about this thick." She showed him with her hands and fingers. "It had the words of God in it. I never read them, of course, but someone read them to me, just a little."

Another old Christian motioned for Yun to come close, so he could whisper. "I was a young man when they had the Bible burnings," he said. "I don't usually talk about it, but I'll tell you. If anyone was found to have a Bible, it would be burned. Then his whole family would be beaten in the middle of the village. Those were terrible days." The old man's body shook as he gazed at the ground. "If you look for a Bible, you're putting yourself in great danger."

But Yun acted as if he hadn't heard the warning. He said, "That means there used to be Bibles before our leader destroyed them. So then, somebody might have a hidden one somewhere right now!" Yun clenched his fists in determination. "I want one!"

15

His words sounded like a cry. "I want to know the words of God! I want to know more about Jesus!"

"Not too loud! Not too loud!" the other people scolded him. "You never know who's listening!"

Day after day Yun talked about it. One day his mother whispered, "Son, I've remembered something important. I remember an old man who used to be a pastor of a church before the Communists took control of our government. They put him in prison for twenty years, but now he's back home in his village. It's about a day's walk from here. He might have a Bible. If he doesn't, he might know how to get one."

Yun's heart leaped up with hope. Together he and his mother started out on the long walk to the other village, trudging the dusty road in their bare feet.

When they arrived, they asked for the house of the man who had been in prison. Fearfully the other villagers pointed to one hut.

The old man looked skinny and weak. When he saw Yun and his mother, his eyes showed fear and suspicion. "What do you want?" he asked.

"Please sir," Yun begged quietly. "I long to see a Bible. Do you have one?"

The old man's body began to shake, and he didn't answer right away. He studied Yun and his mother for several minutes. Their dusty rags. Their bare feet. Their pleading faces.

Finally he spoke in a low and quavering voice. "The Bible is a heavenly book," he said. "You have to ask God for it. He's the only one who can give it to you. If you keep asking Him in faith, He'll give you your heart's desire."

Yun's heart leaped up with hope once again. They had prayed for Father to be healed, and he was. Why hadn't he thought to pray for a Bible? He and Mother hurried back home with renewed energy.

Every night Yun prayed, "Dear God, please give me a Bible. Amen." For more than a month he prayed.

But nothing happened.

Again Yun trudged back to the old pastor's house. Again the old pastor looked fearful.

"I've asked every day for a Bible," Yun told the pastor. "But God hasn't given it to me. Please, don't you have one? Couldn't I just look at it? Couldn't I just copy down some of the Scriptures to take back with me—"

But the old man said, "You need to keep asking God. But this time, don't just pray. You need to fast while you pray. And cry out to Him with tears."

Yun went back home, determined to do what the old pastor had said. He began eating only one small bowl of rice a day. For over three months, he did almost nothing but pray for that Bible, with many tears. "I feel like if I don't get a Bible, I'll die!" he cried. His parents became very worried about him.

Then one night, in the middle of the night, Yun was kneeling beside his bed. While he was there, he had a strange vision from the Lord.

Chapter 3

Living Bread in a Red Bag

In Yun's vision, he saw himself pushing an old empty cart up a steep hill. He was pushing it up to another village, to beg food from them. But how heavy this old cart was! It was so heavy Yun felt sure it was about to roll back over on him.

He struggled and strained, feeling close to tears because life was so hard.

Then in his vision, Yun saw three men coming down the hill toward him. The leader was an old man with a long flowing beard. He held the handles of a cart that followed behind him. The other two walked on both sides of the cart.

The cart was full of red bags. Out of the bags came the smell of freshly baked bread. How good it smelled to the hungry teenager!

The old man with the long beard looked at Yun with eyes full of compassion. "Are you hungry?" he asked. His words sounded so kind that Yun's stopped-up tears began to flow. He choked out the word, "Yes."

In his vision, Yun saw the old man hand one of the red bags to his two helpers. "Give this to the young man," he said. Then he looked at Yun and said, "You must eat it right away."

In his vision Yun eagerly opened the wrapping. He took the bun of fresh bread and put it into his mouth. But in his mouth, to his surprise the bread turned into a Bible!

In his vision Yun cried out, "Worthy Lord, I praise Your Name! You heard my prayer and gave me a Bible! I want to give my whole life to You!"

Suddenly Yun awoke from his vision. There he was, kneeling beside his mat in his little house.

"Where is it?" he murmured. "Where is it?" His vision had been so real, he felt sure the Bible must be somewhere in the house.

But there was no Bible anywhere to be found. "It was only a dream!" Yun cried out. He began to weep loudly.

"Son, what is it? What's wrong?" Yun's mother and father came running.

"I saw something in the night!" Yun tried to explain through his tears. "I received a Bible! Three men came, and gave me bread, and it was really a Bible. I *know* I received a Bible! It has to be here somewhere!" But he put his head down on his arms and cried, because it wasn't there.

Yun's father and mother looked at each other in dismay.

"Son," said Mother gently, "no one has come to our house at all. See, the door is still locked."

Yun's father tightly held his son's shaking body. "Dear Lord!" he prayed. "Please don't let my son go crazy! I'm willing to be sick again if You'll just keep him from losing his mind! O Lord, please give my son a Bible!"

Yun's mother knelt down too. All of them hugged each other and wept loudly.

Suddenly there was a knock on the door.

A man's gentle voice called quietly.

Yun jumped up and ran to the door. He didn't unlock it, but whispered the first question that came to him.

"Are you bringing the bread to me?"

The gentle voice answered. "Yes, we are. We have a feast of bread for you."

It was the voice he had heard in his vision!

Yun quickly unlocked the door. There stood two men. *They were the same as the two servants he had seen in his vision.*

Without a word, one man held out a red bag. Yun took it with trembling hands.

Inside was a Bible.

Without a word, the two men disappeared into the darkness of the night.

Right there in his doorway, Yun went down on his knees, thanking God for his Bible. "Lord, Jesus," he prayed, "from this moment on, I will eat your words like a hungry child eats bread. I will never doubt that they are Your holy words to me. You have answered my prayer!"

୫୦୧୫

Some time later, Yun found out where those two men had come from. They were friends of an old Chinese evangelist who lived in a village far away, a man Yun had never met.

This evangelist had been beaten and nearly killed for his Christian faith. But before he was taken to prison, he had carefully put his Bible inside a metal can and buried it.

One night, three months before Yun's vision, the evangelist had a vision from the Lord too. In it, he saw a certain village and a certain house and a certain young man. The Lord said, "Give your Bible to him."

It took the evangelist three months to finally obey the voice of the Lord. When he did, he asked two of his friends to do the job for him.

Of course, the certain village was Yun's village, the certain house was Yun's house, and the certain young man was Yun himself.

God was faithful to answer prayer.

Chapter 4

"Go West, Go South"

Yun read his Bible all day long, every day. He took it with him everywhere he went. When he worked in the fields, he hid it under his tattered shirt. Then he read it whenever he could. When he finally fell asleep at night, it was with his Bible on his chest.

But reading the Bible was hard for him. For one thing, this teenager had gone to school for only three years. Reading was a struggle. But also, this Bible was written in the old, difficult Chinese writing. Yun had learned the new, simple writing.

It was hard. But Yun got a dictionary and looked up the words as he read. He didn't give up. Finally after a few months he had finished reading the whole thing.

Then he began to memorize the first book of the New Testament, Matthew. He memorized a chapter a day. After a month, he could recite the whole book.

One day Yun was reading in the book of Acts. He read Acts 1:8, which says,

> *But you shall receive power when the Holy Spirit has come upon you; and you shall be witnesses to Me in Jerusalem, and in all Judea and Samaria, and to the end of the earth.*

But who was this Holy Spirit who was going to give this power? Yun didn't know. Had he read about Him in some other part of the Bible? He went to ask his mother.

His mother sighed. "You know I've already told you all I know. I don't know the answers to your questions. But you can ask God for the answers.

And you can ask Him for that Holy Spirit of power, just like you asked Him for your Bible."

Of course he could.

Yun prayed to the Lord, "I need this power. I need Your Holy Spirit. I'm willing to be Your witness."

A great joy and sense of God's love filled the young man. Then the Holy Spirit brought new thoughts to him from all the Scriptures he had been reading and memorizing. Yun had never learned any songs about the Lord, but he began to sing. He felt the joy of the Holy Spirit.

Yun trusted that the power of the Holy Spirit would strengthen him to be a witness.

Then late one evening something happened.

Yun had prayed and finished memorizing Acts 12. He was getting ready to go to sleep.

But he felt a tap on his shoulder and heard a voice.

"Yun! I'm going to send you to be My witness, to the west and south."

Yun jumped out of bed in the dark. Who had said that? Who had tapped his shoulder?

He went to his parents' room. "Did you call me?" he asked. "Did you come into my room and tap me on my shoulder?"

"No, we didn't," said his mother. "Go back to sleep."

Chapter 5

Obeying the Voice in the Night

Yun went back to his room and lay down again on his mat. After a few minutes he heard it again. A clear voice said to him, "Yun, you will be My witness. You will go to the west and south to tell the good news of Jesus Christ."

Once again Yun jumped up. This time he knew it wasn't one of his parents, but he went to their room anyway.

"Mother, I heard a voice. It told me to go to the west and south to take the gospel of Jesus Christ."

"Oh my son." Yun's mother shook her head. "Please try not to be so excited. Try to rest."

Chapter 5

Yun went back to his room and kneeled down by his bed. "Lord Jesus," he prayed, "I'm listening. If You want me to preach for You, I will. I'm ready and willing to obey You."

Then he lay down on his bed and went to sleep.

Very, very early in the morning, before it was light, Yun had a dream. In his dream he saw the old man again, the same old man with the long beard who had the cart with the red bags of bread.

In this dream, the old man came to him. He said, "You need to turn your face to the west and to the south. It is there you will be a witness for the Lord to tell His good news to others."

Suddenly, in the dream, the old man and the teenager faced a large group of people. The old man turned to Yun and said, "You will be the witness to them."

In front of this crowd, Yun felt very small. But then a woman came toward him. She acted strange and threw her body around. Yun knew she had a demon, just like in the book of Acts.

In the dream the old man said, "Lay hands on her and cast out the demon in the name of Jesus."

Yun had never done anything like this, but in his dream he did it. He laid hands on the woman and commanded the demon to come out. The woman's body thrashed, but then she lay still. When she raised her head, Yun saw that she was free. So did everyone else in the crowd! All of them were astonished at this great work the Lord had done.

Then in his dream, Yun's attention was drawn to one young man. "Are you brother Yun?" the young man asked. "My name is Yu Jing Chai, and I'm 24 years old. My people in the south need you to come preach the gospel to us. We've been fasting and praying for you for three days."

Yun's heart was touched. "Tomorrow I'll go with you to your village," he said.

Then he awoke.

As soon as it was light, Yun went to his parents. "I have to go," he said. "I have to go preach the gospel."

"Where are you going?" Mother asked.

"The Lord spoke to me three times last night," Yun answered. "He told me to go west and south to preach the gospel. I have to obey. First I'm going west to preach. But then a young man will come here for me. When he comes, I have to go south with him and preach there. Mother, please tell him to wait for my return."

"What do you mean?" said his mother. "What are you talking about?"

"A young man will be coming from the south," Yun repeated patiently. "His name is Yu Jing Chai, and he is 24 years old. He has on a white shirt and gray pants with patches. The Christians in his village have been fasting and praying for me for three days, so I have to go. The Lord showed me all this in a dream."

Chapter 6

Hungry People in the West

Yun tucked his Bible into his bag. Then he confidently headed toward the west. He didn't know where he was going, but he was sure the Lord would lead him. After all, the Lord had told him three times to go.

As he walked, Yun greeted the people he passed. Would one of them be the person to whom he was sent?

Then one old man stopped him. "Where are you going?" he asked.

Yun replied, "I'm going to the west. The God of heaven came to me three times last night. He told me to take His gospel to the west and south."

Tears came to the old man's eyes. "You're the young man I've come to find," he said. "There are a few Christians in my village in the west. We've heard the secret news from your village. We heard that you prayed to God for a heavenly book and received it. We've been fasting and praying for you for three days. I'm here to ask you to come and tell us what the heavenly book says."

God did it! He connected Yun with the very person he needed to meet! Yun and the old Christian walked to the village together.

All the people were working in the fields. The old man called to them, "Come! This is the young man we've been praying for!"

The people dropped their tools in the field and came running. Thirty or forty of them crammed into one small house. Many had heard the strange story of how Yun had received his Bible. All of them fixed their eyes on this young man. All of them expected something.

The sixteen-year-old looked around. *How can I speak to all these people?* he wondered. *How can I give them what they need?*

Suddenly he squeezed his eyes tight shut. He held his precious Bible high above his head. "This is the Bible, the heavenly book!" he shouted. "The God of heaven answered my prayers by sending it to me. If you want one, you must pray and seek God the way I did."

He opened his eyes. All the people were gazing at him in wonder. Then someone spoke. "Please teach us from it."

But Yun didn't know how to teach. He had no idea what it meant to teach anyone from the Word of God. So instead, he closed his eyes again and began to recite the gospel of Matthew. He recited all 28 chapters, without stopping.

When he finished, he didn't open his eyes just yet. The Holy Spirit gave him some songs to sing, based on the book of Matthew. One song was about rejoicing greatly when we're persecuted for the sake of the gospel. Another was about how we should never deny our Master the way Judas did.

When Yun finished singing, he opened his eyes. All over the room, people were in tears, kneeling and weeping. The Word of God and the Holy Spirit had come in power.

Chapter 7

Young Man from the South

All the people in that room cried out to God. They asked God to forgive their sins. They asked God to save them through the blood of Jesus Christ. They believed that Jesus loved them, died for them, and rose again for them.

Yun knew this power was from the Holy Spirit. He knew the Spirit was using the Word of God in people's hearts. They were seeing Jesus.

For a long time the people prayed and rejoiced. Then some of them said, "Please give us more of God's words."

"I can't," Yun replied sadly. "I have to go. God told me I also need to be His witness in the south."

"Please, please stay just a little while longer," they said. "Please give us just a little more!"

So Yun stayed. He recited the first twelve chapters of the book of Acts.

"That's all I've learned," he said. "I need to memorize more. Then I'll come and recite it to you."

As Yun prepared to leave, a young woman came up to him. "You mentioned you were going to the south," she said. "Which village are you going to?"

"I don't know the name of the village," Yun replied. "But when I get home, a young man will be there. His name is Yu Jing Chai. He'll take me to his village."

The woman was startled. "Do you know him?" she asked.

"Yes, I do."

"How did you meet him?"

"I met him in a dream from the Lord early this morning," Yun said.

Tears came to the young woman's eyes. "He's my brother!" she said. "Yu Jing Chai is my brother! After I believed in the Lord Jesus, I told my mother and my brother about Him. And they believed too. We've all been fasting and praying for the young man who has the heavenly book."

෨෬

When Yun finally returned home, his mother greeted him. "The young man came here," she said with joy. "The one you told me about!"

"But I said to keep him here until I returned!" Yun answered, distressed. "I'm supposed to go with him to his village! But he's gone."

"But son, listen to my story," Mother continued. "He came, exactly as you said. He was dressed just as you described. I said, 'Is your name Yu Jing Chai?' He was startled and asked how I knew. I said, 'You came to ask my son to go preach the gospel in your village in the south, didn't you?' Then he was amazed. I told him about your dream. And I told him you would return by sunset. He said he would be back at the same time."

And there he came, just as the sun was setting. Yun walked with Yu Jing Chai to the south. He told him all about his dream and his day in the village in the west. He told Yu about meeting his sister in the other village.

Late in the evening they reached Yu's village. It was after dark, but many people were gathered. Again Yun recited all of the book of Matthew and the first twelve chapters of Acts. Again he sang the Scripture songs he had learned from the Holy Spirit.

The fire of God caught hold in the villages to the west and to the south.

❦

The Lord worked mightily through Brother Yun even while he was a teenager. Before he turned eighteen, he had seen over two thousand people believe on Jesus Christ. They were hungry for the Living Bread.

The Communist authorities began to find out about the new Christians in the area around Yun's village. They arrested them and demanded who had told them about Jesus.

But the Christians refused to betray their Lord the way Judas had. Instead, they rejoiced to be persecuted for the Name of their Savior.

Chapter 8

The Black Evil of Death

Through the next few years, more and more people came to Jesus for salvation. Then some Christians from Western countries smuggled in a million Bibles. The house churches were growing. The leaders of the Communist government didn't know what to do.

So the police began to work harder than ever. They hunted for those "house church" Christians. They wanted to beat them or put them in prison. They even wanted to kill them.

Just like in the book of Acts, this persecution made the Christians flee to other villages. Wherever they fled, they took the gospel.

ಹಿ ೦೪

One evening in 1983, 25-year-old Brother Yun prayed with a group of friends. They were getting ready to leave their province of Henan. The gospel needed to go to a new place in the west. Many of the people in those mountains had never even seen outsiders.

As the friends prayed, Brother Yun suddenly cried out. Then he shouted, "Hallelujah! Jesus' blood has overcome you!"

Everyone looked up, startled. "What's wrong?" they asked. "What happened?"

Brother Yun opened his eyes. He touched his forehead, feeling the sweat. "I had a terrible vision," he said. "A dark, evil, ugly creature came against me. It pushed me down and sat on me. Then it grabbed me by the throat and started choking me. It grabbed some sort of tool and used it to try to hold my mouth shut.

"Then I saw something else. An angel of the Lord flew toward me, big and white. I poked out the eyes of the black creature, and it fell over. Then the angel took me and carried me away. That was when I shouted, 'Hallelujah! Jesus' blood has overcome you!'"

The other Christians listened in wonder. They knew there was much danger in their work. They knew the forces of evil would come against them. But they also knew that the power of God was stronger.

They prayed some more, trusted the Lord, and shared the Lord's supper together.

The next day Brother Yun and his friends left for the mountain area. A few Christians welcomed them there. Others came to hear him speak. The whole first day, Yun preached the gospel. But the second day after lunch he lost his voice. He went to a room to rest.

While he was resting, something dark and evil happened.

Three men in uniforms burst into the room. One of the men threw him onto the bed. Then he sat on top of him. He put his hand round Brother Yun's throat. Then he pulled out an ID badge. "I'm from the government," he growled.

Brother Yun remembered his vision. This was what God had warned him about! But there was no need to fear, because the angel of God would come.

The other two men in uniforms got out some ropes. They roughly pulled Yun's arms behind his back. As they were tying him up, one of them saw a wooden cross on the wall. The cross said, "For God so loved the world." "He hung on the cross." And "He took our sins upon Himself."

When the officers saw that cross, they laughed a loud and evil laugh. "Let's tie it on his back!" one said. So they did. The arms of the cross stuck out so that anyone could read what it said.

"What a fool you are!" they laughed.

Chapter 9

Jesus from Henan

The government officers kicked Yun, hit him, and spat upon him.

"Please!" cried the owner of the house. "This is a good man. He has done nothing wrong!"

"We know what he's done," growled one of the officers. "He has broken the law by preaching that Jesus!" He jerked at Yun's shirt. "Where are you from?"

"Henan," Yun replied. But then he realized he shouldn't have told that. He didn't want to get anyone there in trouble. He decided not to say another word.

Chapter 9

The officers forced Yun to walk to the middle of town in front of their car. Behind him, from the car's loudspeaker, they shouted, "This man came here from Henan to preach Jesus. He has confused the people. He has disturbed the peace. But we've captured him and will punish him."

People came running from all over. "Who is it? Who's there?" They gasped to see a man tied up with ropes with a cross on his back. "Did he say it's Jesus from Henan? What does that wooden thing say?"

The officers made Yun kneel down on the ground. With their heavy boots they kicked him and kicked him, because he preached about Jesus. Then they made him get up and trudge through another street. They mocked him over the loudspeaker again.

Yun looked up. By now, a great crowd of people had gathered. Some of them stared in disbelief. Some mocked, shouting "Jesus from Henan!" But some of them had tears in their eyes at the way this man was being treated.

"Please," Yun was able to whisper. "Don't weep for me. Weep for the lost souls of China."

Then the people in the crowd cried even harder.

When night came, the officers took Brother Yun to the police station. Many people followed and stood outside the window, staring in. The officers took off the cross, but kept him tightly bound with the ropes.

"What is your name?" the angry officer shouted.

Yun didn't want to get any of his fellow believers in trouble, so he didn't say a word. He lay on the floor and let his eyes roll back into his head. Slobber started dripping out of his mouth.

The onlookers at the window gasped.

"What's wrong with this man? Is he crazy?" The officers backed off, frightened.

"I'll call Henan province," said the head officer. "I'm sure they can tell us who he is." He went into the next room to make a phone call, and all the other officers followed him. All the onlookers moved to that window, to watch the officer make the phone call.

Now Yun was all alone. No one was watching. It was at that moment he heard the voice of the Lord. "The God of Peter is your God." Yun remembered how an angel had helped Peter escape from prison.

Then he felt the ropes that held his hands tied behind his back. They snapped apart.

Chapter 10

Delivered from the Black Evil of Death

Yun listened. Yes, the officers were still on the phone in the other room. Behind his back, he tried moving his hands a little. Yes, they could move.

It was time to get up and walk out of that police station.

Keeping his arms behind him as if the ropes were still tight, Yun stood up. With his mouth he tried to work the doorknob.

The door swung open. He was in the hallway.

The blood of Jesus has overcome them! he thought to himself. He kept walking.

Out into the courtyard he walked. The people out there barely even glanced at him.

Yun kept walking, to the corner of the courtyard. He looked up at the wall: eight feet high, with sharp glass in the top.

Yun climbed up enough that he could peer over the wall. On the other side was a pit, ten feet wide.

What would he do? How would he get over it to the other side?

Suddenly Yun felt as if someone picked him up and threw him over the wall. He landed on the far side of the pit.

It was the angel of the Lord.

Yun remembered the Scripture in Psalm 18:29,

For by You I can run against a troop;

by my God I can leap over a wall.

God had delivered him! He was on the other side!

Darkness had fallen now, and Yun started running. He was only visiting this province of China and didn't know the area at all. He didn't know which way to go. He just started running. He ran and ran. He fell down and got up again and kept running. For hours he ran, climbing over a mountain, crossing a river, and climbing over another mountain.

Then in the moonlight someone called to him.

"Brother Yun? Where are you going?" The man came closer. "Brother Yun! What's happened to you?"

"Who are you?" Yun asked, gasping for breath. "How do you know me? Do you believe in Jesus?"

"I came to your meetings all day yesterday," said the farmer. "I came this morning too, but then you lost your voice. So I came back to my fields to keep on working. Now I'm working late at night to catch up on yesterday's work."

"And you're here." Brother Yun breathed deeply again and again. "And I'm here."

The Lord had done it once again.

"But what happened?" the farmer asked.

"Didn't you hear anything about it?"

"No," answered the farmer. "I've just been here working my crops and haven't seen anyone."

"Officers from the government came this afternoon," Yun explained, "right after I lost my voice. They took me prisoner, but the Lord rescued me from them. Can you take me back to see your church leaders and my fellow workers?"

Immediately the farmer put down his tools and walked with Brother Yun the long path back to the house church.

As they approached the house, they could hear voices.

"Rescue him, O Lord!" they were crying. "Deliver him from the hands of bloody men! For the sake of Your gospel! For the sake of Your Name!"

Brother Yun and the farmer approached the door and knocked.

When they came inside, the Christians gasped and ran to the door. "He has done it! The Lord has answered our prayers!"

But they saw that Brother Yun had been badly beaten. Gently they bathed his wounds and tended his sores and his dark purple bruises.

As they cared for him with tears, Brother Yun encouraged them. "Remember that Jesus said we would suffer for Him. We can learn to rejoice through suffering as we see the Kingdom of God grow. Some people who saw me trudging through the streets will never forget this day. They saw the cross that said 'God so loved the world.' They'll want to know more about this God. Stand faithful and true, brothers and sisters, even in persecution."

"We will," the believers promised. "Thank you for showing us what it means to be a Christian. We want to follow in this path."

Chapter 11

The Heavenly Man

"This is a dangerous criminal!" all the posters announced. "Whoever helps catch him will receive a great reward!" On each poster was the face of 25-year-old Brother Yun. The posters were pasted all over Yun's part of Henan province. Surely his life was in danger.

Yun went to visit the Christians in a far northern province. In this area, no one knew that he was a "dangerous criminal."

But government officers stood at the edge of the village. They knew this stranger looked suspicious.

"Who are you?" The officers grabbed Yun and threw him to the ground. "Where are you from? What are you doing here? Where are your other workers? Tell us the truth or we'll kill you!"

Yun looked up at the officers. Several of the other Christians were still in the house. Maybe if he shouted loudly enough they would hear him. Then they could escape.

He began to throw his arms about wildly. "I am a heavenly man!" he shouted. "My father's name is Abundant Blessing! I live in Gospel Village!"

"What are you talking about?" the officers roared. They kicked him and shoved him.

"I'm not from this earth!" Yun continued to shout. "I'm a heavenly man! I'm a heavenly man! The heavenly man will never become a Judas!"

The brothers and sisters in the house church heard his yelling. At first they followed him in their love for him. Four of the other pastors were captured. But the other Christians ran away to safety.

The officers put handcuffs on Brother Yun and the others. They marched them back to the police station. In the freezing cell, Yun beat on a little drum. He shouted Psalm 150.

Praise the Lord! . . .

Praise Him for His mighty acts.

Praise Him according to His excellent greatness!

Praise Him with the sound of the trumpet.

Praise Him with the lute and harp!

Praise Him with the timbrel and dance.

Praise Him with stringed instruments and

Praise Him with loud cymbals.

Praise Him with clashing cymbals!

Let everything that has breath praise the Lord.

Praise the Lord!

As he sang, his hands and feet became warm. His heart filled with joy. He crouched down on the freezing cell floor, along with the other Christian men. Together they prayed for God to save China.

Weeks later, the authorities from Yun's part of Henan province finally came. "You got him!" they shouted gleefully. "You caught one of the most wanted criminals in all of Henan province!"

These officers beat Yun so badly he thought he would die. But the Lord spoke to his heart.

You are sharing in my suffering. Be still and know that I am God. I will be exalted in the nations. I will be exalted in the earth. Be still and know that I am God.

The fear and pain left him.

When they reached Yun's hometown, the police slowed down their car. They turned on their siren so all the people would come. Then they spoke through the loudspeakers.

"Cheer for the government officers!" the police announced. "We have good news for all the people of the town! We've captured the terrible criminal Yun, who held illegal meetings. We must stand against all illegal Christian meetings!"

The officers carried Yun into the police station. "This is the day you have lost and we have won!"

they boasted. "Your church is finished! You have failed! Tell us who the other Christians are!"

But Yun refused to be a Judas.

Chapter 12

Great Work of God in Prison

The Lord told Brother Yun to stay silent and still and trust Him. Day after day the guards and even the other prisoners mocked him. They beat him and treated him terribly, nearly killing him.

Whenever he could, Yun spoke to the other prisoners about Jesus Christ. But he refused to betray his fellow Christians.

He also refused to eat. For weeks and weeks he didn't take a bite of food. His body became skinnier and smaller. Then he stopped speaking.

The other prisoners continued to mock Yun and treat him cruelly.

After weeks of not eating, Yun weighed only 66 pounds. But the Lord sustained him. God gave him many precious promises from all the Scripture he had memorized.

Finally Yun's mother, wife, and other relatives were allowed to visit. They brought bread and grape juice. For the first time in over two months, Yun took some food. He took the Lord's supper with them.

"Son," Yun's mother whispered. "The Lord has told me you will not die. You will stay alive for God!"

When she was leaving, Yun suddenly shouted out to her. "Mother, preach the gospel! Ask the churches to fast and pray for me!"

It was the first time he had spoken in weeks.

When Yun returned to his cell block, the guard and all the prisoners there mocked him. "How dare you do this!" The guard shouted. "You finally eat and drink and speak after all this time! I will kill you!"

One of the prisoners snarled, "You're dying like a sick dog because you believe in Jesus."

"You deserve to die," said another. "You're preaching Jesus against our nation's laws."

For weeks Yun hadn't spoken. For weeks he hadn't been strong enough to walk.

But now suddenly the Holy Spirit of power came upon him. He stood up.

"I have a message from the Lord for you!" Yun declared. "Listen to me!"

This tiny man looked like a small skeleton. The prisoners were astonished that he could speak with such power.

"God sent me here for you," Yun continued. "You knew from the first day that I am a Christian pastor. That first day you heard me speak of His love and salvation. Now you know I've been fasting for 74 days.

"But now my Lord has filled me with power. Now I stand here and tell you that Jesus is the true and living God. You must stop your sin and evil!

The judgment day is coming! How will you escape hell? You must cry out to Jesus for His forgiveness! He is the only one who can save you! This day He offers you His great mercy and salvation! You must confess your sins! You must repent! You must ask God to forgive you! Kneel before Him. There is no other hope!"

All the men were thunderstruck. At first none of them could say a word.

Then the leader of the cell block fell on his knees. He was the man who had been most cruel to Yun. "What can I do to be saved?" he cried.

Then the others knelt too, even one who was a Muslim. "How can we be forgiven of our many sins?" they cried.

With tears these wicked men called out for the merciful Lord to save them. They asked Him to wash them clean and make them new. A prison guard heard the noise and came running. He too stood amazed.

The whole cell block was changed. All the men were so sorry for the way they had treated Brother Yun. Now when they went out into the prison yard, they wanted to tell the other prisoners about Jesus.

Together they shared their tiny bits of food. Together they prayed for the people they had hurt. They prayed for the families of those they had killed. Together they listened to the gospel proclaimed by the heavenly man.

Chapter 13

Madman in Prison

"Yun, I have an assignment for you." The director of the prison looked at this small skinny man that he couldn't control. "I'm going to send a violent murderer to your cell. I'm warning you, he's crazy. He tries to bite the other prisoners. He tries to hurt and even kill himself."

Yun's heart swelled with love for this prisoner.

"One time he punched his head into the cement block wall," the director continued. "He left a dent in the wall." He waited for the look of surprise to pass from Yun's face. "He's going to be executed for his many crimes. But before that time comes, he's not allowed to kill himself. And he's not allowed to hurt anyone else. If he does, you'll be responsible. His name is Huang, and he's just 22 years old."

"I was also 22 years old when I was arrested the first time," Yun murmured. But his arrest had been for preaching the gospel of Jesus Christ.

When Yun returned to his cell block, he told his friends. They were frightened. "That man Huang— I've heard about him!" said one. "He's like ... like ... an animal."

"He's like a devil," said someone else. The others agreed.

"But my brothers," said Yun. "Without Christ, we're all just like him. Don't any of you remember your former lives?"

Some of the men grunted and looked down.

"In the other cell block, the other prisoners have treated Huang exactly like this," Brother Yun continued. "They treated him like an animal. They wanted him to die. But without Jesus, all of us are just as lost as this man. We can show him the same mercy our Savior has shown us."

The hearts of the men changed. They looked forward to welcoming Huang.

When Huang came, he seemed like a man who was demon possessed. He was tied with chains on his wrists and ankles, but he still tried to hurt anyone who came near. He also tried to hurt himself. He snarled and spoke the most disgusting speech he could. His clothes and body matched his language—filthy.

But Huang was no match for the love of God. He was about to meet that love in this cell block.

"Sit down," Brother Yun said gently. "We won't hurt you. We want to help you. Brothers, will you share some of your water so we can help Huang be clean?"

Huang watched without a word. The men of the cell took their small cups of water. Each one poured a little of their precious water into a basin. Yun used part of his shirt to clean Huang's dirty, bloody face. Then he tore off part of his blanket. He used it to gently wash Huang's open sores.

At lunchtime, each prisoner gave Huang a bit of his rice. Yun fed him with a spoon. Huang sat without saying a word. He couldn't understand men who would act in such a way.

After lunch the men all sang a song together about God's love and care. Then Brother Yun taught them all from Matthew 6.

Once a week each prisoner was given a small roll of bread with their supper. Tonight was the night. Brother Yun started to eat all his roll, but the Spirit of God stopped him. He ate only part of it and saved the rest to share with Huang later.

The next morning when the guard brought some watery soup, all the prisoners shared with Huang once again. But he spoke up loudly. "This isn't enough food!" he yelled at the guard. "Do you want me to starve before you execute me?"

Brother Yun knew from the Lord that it was time to share his bread. He pulled out his small roll. Then he tore it into bits, putting the pieces in Huang's soup bowl.

At that moment, Huang's heart broke. He began to weep and fell to his knees. "Older brother," he cried, "why do you treat me with such kindness? Why do you love me like this?"

Yun knew Huang's heart was ready for the gospel. "It is the love of Jesus Christ that fills us," he said. "If not for the love of Christ, we would be the same as the men in your other cell. God has given His Son Jesus Christ for you."

"Thank You, God!" Huang cried out. "Thank You for loving me. You have loved me even though I'm a terrible sinner. I want to receive the great love of Jesus Christ!"

.

Chapter 14

I Don't Want Your Money!

Huang had been a criminal. He had done many evil, wicked things. But now he was just like the other prisoners in Yun's cell block. He wanted to know more about Jesus!

As Yun taught Huang, he grew in the Lord. This became his favorite song:

I love Jesus. I love Jesus.

Every day of my life I love Jesus.

When days are sunny I love him.

When the storm clouds gather I love him.

Every day along my way,

Yes, I love Jesus.

Huang knew he was going to be executed for his crimes. But he wanted to live his last few days for the Lord. He told many other prisoners about Him before he was finally put to death.

Before he died, Huang wrote a letter to his father and mother.

Dear Papa and Mama,

I have dishonored you, but I know you still love me. After I'm dead, please don't be sad. I have some wonderful news. I have received eternal life! In prison I met a man named Brother Yun. He loved me and cared for me. He helped me to believe in Jesus Christ, so I'm on my way to heaven.

Papa and Mama, I will pray for you. You must believe in Jesus! I'm praying that you will receive eternal life. I want to see you in heaven. Please let Brother Yun tell you the good news about Jesus.

ೞೞ

After four years of imprisonment, in 1988 Yun was finally released. He praised God and rejoiced to be with his family again. Then he went back to preaching the gospel wherever he could.

One of his first visits was to Huang's parents. They were both members of the Communist party and of very high rank.

"Your sons' body is dead," Yun told them. "But his spirit is alive in heaven with Jesus Christ. His last request was that you trust in the Savior too."

Yun talked with them for hours. They saw how important it was to believe. But oh, the cost would be so great for them. They would lose their high standing in Chinese society.

Finally Huang's father pulled out a big pile of money. He handed it to Yun. "Thank you for your trouble," he said. "Thank you for coming."

Yun stood up, his eyes flashing. He took the money and threw it down on the table. "I don't want your money!" he commanded. "I want your souls! In the holy Name of the Lord Jesus Christ, I command you to kneel down and take Him as your Savior!"

Both of them immediately went down on their knees. They both began to weep before the Lord, confessing their sins.

That day Huang's parents trusted in Jesus Christ. Since then they have continued as faithful disciples of their King. Huang's last wish was granted.

Chapter 15

Exalted Like Joseph

From 1988 to 1991 Brother Yun and his wife Deling and the other Christians preached the gospel all over China. Thousands of people came to Christ.

But the Lord warned Yun that he needed to stop and rest. Deling even had a dream about it. She was sure another arrest was coming and they needed to escape. But Yun ignored her.

Four days later, Yun was arrested.

"O heavenly Lord, forgive me!" he prayed. "I was proud and stubborn. I wouldn't listen to the warning You gave through my wife! Forgive me!" he wept bitter tears of repentance.

But he was sentenced to three years in a labor camp.

"Watch this man well!" the government officials told the camp director. "He's a dangerous criminal. He turns the other prisoners against the government, and he tries to escape. Watch him well!"

The director of the labor camp was afraid. He ordered Yun to stay silent and not speak a word.

For several days Yun didn't speak. The guards and the other prisoners didn't know what his crime was. They thought he must have murdered or done something else terrible. They beat him again and again. But Yun remained silent.

His heart was broken. He was broken over his own sin. "God forgive me!" he prayed. "I won't try to escape this time. I know this imprisonment is a time for You to teach me."

And his heart was broken over the needs of the men he saw around him. Many of the prisoners had so little food they could barely move. They just lay on the floor waiting to die. "Lord, make a way for me to be able to give them the gospel!"

One day Yun saw a sick prisoner moaning in his cell, and felt compassion for him. He knew it was time to break his silence. He said to the guard, "I know how to help pain. Will you allow me to massage that man's shoulders?"

"You do?" said the guard. "Go ahead. But don't try any tricks. I'm watching you."

Yun leaned over and gently began to rub the sick man's shoulders. Then he whispered in his ear. "My friend, Jesus Christ is the way to peace. Trust in Him. He is your only hope! He died for you, and He loves you."

The prisoner's eyes flew open. What new words were these?

Yun was allowed to give massages to other men too. To each one, he gave the gospel. The prisoners began coming to Christ.

The guards saw nothing dangerous. In fact, all the prisoners were becoming more peaceful. They were better workers. "You're not saying anything against the government, are you, Yun?" one guard asked suspiciously.

"Not at all," answered Yun. "I'm simply giving them hope and freedom from pain."

"Huh," grunted the guard. "There's nothing wrong with that."

One day Brother Yun had a small group of men gathered around him. He was telling them the truth about Jesus and His great salvation. His face shone with the love of the Lord.

One guard said to another, "He's happier than we are, and he's the prisoner!"

"Ah, but I'm free in my heart," Yun responded. "And I have great hope in Christ."

"Sing us one of your songs," said one of the guards.

Yun promptly began singing. A few of the other prisoners joined him.

Let the world know I have a Savior.

His Name, His Name is Jesus!

The men of the prison learned to love to sing songs of their Savior. In a world without hope, how amazing it was to find out that God loved them!

೮೦೪

"Yun, my neck is sore," the prison camp director said one day. "I heard you can do a good job of helping pain with your massage. Will you massage my neck for me?"

"Gladly," said Brother Yun. While he did, he spoke gently to the director about the love of God through Jesus Christ.

"Yun, the government officials told us you were a dangerous criminal. But we've been watching you closely for months. You obey everything we tell you to do. You don't cause any trouble. You encourage the other prisoners. You even helped my neck feel better!" The director turned his neck from side to side.

"So I want to tell you something. I'm going to make you the leader of your cell block. You'll be in charge of making sure all the prisoners do all their work well. And of course make sure they behave."

This was a privilege. Yun knew most cell leaders did their job by terrorizing the other prisoners. He knew his cell would be different.

As time passed, Yun's cell proved to be the best group in the prison. Then the director called him in again.

"We'd like for you to help in the office here. You can help organize the books. You can help plan the educational programs. You can choose the music we play over the loudspeaker."

Instead of being tortured and persecuted the way he had been in the first prison, now, like Joseph, Yun was exalted.

Chapter 16

Dr. Yun, Massage Expert

One day Yun was busy working in the office. He had turned on the radio to play over the loudspeaker, but it was playing Christian songs.

"Yun, come here now!" called a voice.

Yun jumped and ran out the door. Was he in trouble for playing Christian music over the loudspeaker?

There was the prison camp director. He stood with a doctor from a nearby medical clinic. "Yun is very obedient," said the director. "He works hard and always comes as soon as I call."

The doctor nodded. "I've heard you're an expert at massage," she said. "Where were you trained?"

Yun's heart stopped racing. He was relieved to know he wasn't in trouble!

"I wasn't trained at a massage school," he replied. "I'm a Christian who loves the Lord and wants to help people with their pain."

"Well," said the doctor, "I've heard of your skill. I want to ask you to come to my home to help my father. Half of his body is paralyzed. We hope his great pain can be helped with massage."

Yun heard the Holy Spirit telling him to go. "That would be an honor," he replied. "You'll have my word I won't try to escape."

The next day the doctor took Yun to her family home. There they presented him with fresh fruit and other special foods.

"Thank you," he said. "But I can't eat it. I'm fasting and praying for the Lord to give your father a special blessing."

The doctor's mother was so touched by this that tears came to her eyes.

"I must return to the hospital," said the doctor.

"You don't need to worry," Brother Yun assured her. "I won't try to escape. I'll do what I can to help your father."

The doctor left him alone with her parents. Brother Yun looked at them. "Before I begin with your massage," he said, "I have something I must tell you."

The old man in the bed and his old wife both looked at him expectantly.

"The God of heaven sent His Son Jesus Christ to earth. Out of love for the people of the world, He died on the cross. On the cross He bore your sins and sicknesses."

The old man and his wife raised their eyebrows in surprise. They asked questions, and Brother Yun answered them.

"Now speak!" he said. "Believe with your heart, and confess with your mouth that Jesus Christ is

Lord of your life. Trust Him to save you of your sins and sicknesses. He will bring you great joy and great hope!"

As Yun laid his hands on the old man and the old woman, they began to weep. They confessed their sins. They asked Jesus to save them and use them and be glorified in their lives.

"Is your pain better, sir?" Yun asked.

"No, not yet," replied the old man.

"It will be soon." Yun spoke with confidence. "God will do this work."

The next morning the prison camp director called again. "Yun! Come now!"

Again the doctor stood there.

"Yun!" she said. "Last night my father thanked me for bringing 'Doctor Yun' from the hospital."

"He thought I was a doctor?" Yun asked.

"Yes! And this morning, early, he felt something snap in his neck, like ropes being broken. He can move his neck freely now! Please come join us for breakfast. We all want to thank God together."

Before long, the doctor's father could even walk up and down the stairs. Not only was he free of pain, but he was no longer paralyzed! He and his wife told all their friends about Jesus.

Even the head of the Prison Camp Committee found out that Yun had a gift for helping people with their pain. They decided to pay for Yun to go to massage school.

While he was in prison, Brother Yun became a trained massage expert. He began to work in the medical clinic. There he gave massages to hundreds of people, even high-ranking government officials. He always told them about Jesus. Then his clients invited him to their homes, where he gave the gospel to their families and friends.

ॐ〇ॐ

After two years in prison, Yun was released once more. This time he didn't make the same mistake of jumping right back into the same preaching work again. This time instead, he and Deling spent hours seeking the Lord, asking Him what to do.

God told them He wanted them to start a training school for young believers. They began training young Christians—in a cave! These young believers learned to pray in faith. They became strong in the Lord and in the power of His might.

Chapter 17

"There's No Way You'll Escape Now!"

"Yun, I'm so sick of hearing about you." The judge in the courtroom glared at the prisoner. Yun had been caught yet again in another house church.

"You've taught against our government. For years you've done this! You're turning our whole country upside down with your teachings."

Brother Yun stood quietly, his hands tied behind his back.

"You don't even think it's wrong to disobey the government by escaping," the judge snarled. He glared down at Yun's wounded feet. "This time you tried to escape by jumping out a window! But it didn't work."

Then the judge continued. "Tell me the truth. If you have a chance to escape again, will you take that chance?"

Yun was silent for a moment. He looked at the judge. "I'll answer truthfully, your honor," he said. "God has called me to preach the gospel of Jesus Christ. He wants me to preach it all over my country. I must obey Him. If I have another chance to escape, I'll take it."

Throughout the courtroom rose a murmur of surprise.

"How dare you answer me that way!" the judge roared. "I'll make sure you can *never* escape! Guards!"

The guards stood to attention.

"Take this man and break his legs! Break them so he'll never be able to use them again!"

The guards dragged Yun to another room. There they beat his legs until the bones were crushed. His legs turned black with bruises. As they hit him, they laughed. Let him try to escape now!

Then the guards took Brother Yun to a maximum security prison. No one had *ever* escaped from this prison. Let him try to escape now!

The year was 1997. Now Christians around the world could learn what was happening in China. A message went out all over the world. Brother Yun and other Christian leaders had been imprisoned again. Many Christians around the world began to pray for their release.

Week after week the cruel beatings and mocking continued.

"Hey, Crazy Cripple Man," called a guard. "Are you going to spend the rest of your life in prison?"

"No!" said Brother Yun. "As soon as the Lord says it's time for me to go, I'll go."

Even in his pain, Yun gave the gospel to other men in the prison. But secretly he sometimes cried out to God. "Lord, how could You do this to me?

Why are You letting me rot here in prison?" In his pain he struggled greatly, but he remembered Psalm 27:1.

The Lord is my light and my salvation. Whom shall I fear? The Lord is the strength of my life. Of whom shall I be afraid?

Yun didn't have a Bible in prison. For many days he lay in agony. But the Lord brought him many words of hope from Scriptures he had memorized.

Another pastor, Pastor Zu, was being held in the same prison. He had the job of carrying Brother Yun to the outside toilet. During this time the two pastors could encourage one another. But Pastor Zu kept saying something that made no sense. Several times he whispered to Brother Yun, "I believe the Lord wants you to escape from here."

"Brother," Yun whispered back. "My legs don't work. I can't even stand up. Maybe you're the one who's supposed to escape."

Yun lay in that prison day after day for six weeks. Then one morning the Lord clearly brought a Scripture to his mind. It was Hebrews 10:35.

Do not cast away your confidence, which has great reward.

Then Yun remembered words from Jeremiah 15:11.

Surely I will deliver you for a good purpose.

And then Jeremiah 15:21.

I will deliver you from the hand of the wicked; I will redeem you from the grip of the terrible.

Immediately after that, Yun had a clear vision. In his vision he saw his wife Deling. She was lovingly treating his wounds. Then she looked right at him. "Why don't you open the iron door?" she asked. Then she walked away, and the vision ended.

Right after that, Yun heard the voice of the Lord. *"This is the hour of your salvation."*

Immediately Brother Yun called for the guard. "I need help to go to the toilet," he said. His legs were still black with bruises. Trying to stand on them still caused great agony. He could only crawl a little, by holding on to the wall.

"Hey, Zu," the guard called the other pastor. "Go carry Cripple to the toilet."

Brother Zu came in. But before Brother Yun could say a word, he whispered urgently. "You must escape. The Lord has told me you must escape!"

That was three times in the same morning! The Lord had showed Yun through the Scripture, through his vision, and now through the words of his pastor friend.

Yun knew what he needed to do.

Between him and freedom stood several huge iron gates and many guards with guns.

"I will obey You, Lord," Yun whispered. "I'll try to escape. But the guards are going to shoot me. When they do, I pray that You will receive my soul."

Chapter 18

The Lord Has Done Great Things for Us

It was eight o'clock in the morning. This was the time of the most activity in the prison. It was the very worst time to try to escape.

Yun set his mind on obeying God. With each step, he prayed. "Lord when they shoot me, receive my soul."

He came to the first iron gate. This one opened only from the other side, for people to come in. But just at that time, another prisoner was coming in. The guard with him was suddenly called away to take a phone call. Yun walked out, and the guard didn't notice him.

The second gate stood open because of all the activity in and out. But an armed guard sat watching it carefully.

This was the time the Holy Spirit said, "Go now! The God of Peter is your God!" Yun kept walking. He thought any second he would be shot in the back. But the guard didn't seem to see him.

In the prison yard, about thirty prison guards stood here and there. Yun walked right past them. Didn't they notice him?

The third gate, the gate that was always locked, stood unlocked. Yun walked through.

The front gate was the one that went out to the street. This one was the most heavily guarded. Surely at least two guards would be on duty here.

But no, there were no guards to be seen, and this gate also stood open. Yun walked right out into the street.

Immediately a taxi drove up to him. "Where can I take you?" the driver asked.

Yun climbed in the car. He gave the address of a Christian family in the area and said, "I need to get there very quickly for important business. Don't stop for any reason."

Then he sat back and closed his eye. Had all of this really happened? Only a few moments before, he had been lying in his prison cell!

Soon Yun arrived at the home of the Christian family. They were expecting him! One of them said, "Our church has been fasting and praying for you and your co-workers. Yesterday the Holy Spirit spoke to my mother. He said, 'I will release Yun tomorrow. He will come to your house.' So my parents told us to expect you. We have a secret place for you to hide. It's not far from here."

They took a bicycle to the hiding place. The family member rode on the back while Yun pedaled. All over town the police were setting up barricades to catch the escaped criminal. To avoid them, Brother Yun pedaled down back alleys with his strong legs.

His legs . . . his legs? . . . *His legs!* This was the first time he had realized that his legs were healed! Up until now, he was only thinking about obeying God, and getting shot, and doing the next thing.

Now he realized God had healed his legs!

As soon as they got to the secret place, a terrible rainstorm poured down. The sky turned black. The wind whipped over trash cans and bicycles and anything else in the way. But Brother Yun was safe in his hiding place.

Every day, someone from the family was there. "The police are searching every house and car for you," they whispered. "They're even using trained tracking dogs. But God washed away your scent in that storm. They won't find you here."

Weeks earlier the judge had sneered to Brother Yun. "There's no way you'll escape now!"

But God loves to show Himself powerful before those who mock His Name.

୫୦ଓଷ

The same morning Yun escaped from prison, Yun's wife also had a vision. In it, she saw that her husband was free. "How did you get out of prison?" she asked in the vision.

"The Lord helped me come out," he replied. "Now I must go preach the gospel."

Deling was sure her husband was free. She told her friends. But they thought her grief had made her crazy.

Deling ignored their mockery. She took a bus to the city where her husband had been imprisoned. There she stopped to visit some Christian friends.

"Did you hear that Yun escaped?" the Christian leader asked.

"What? Really?" Deling asked. "Are you sure?"

"Yes, the Christian family who is helping him told us. They said he would come visit us tonight."

Then Deling told them about the vision she had received just that morning. "This is why I'm here," she said.

The Christian leader laughed. "Our heavenly Father's communication is much better than telephones or computers, isn't it?" he said.

That very night Brother Yun was re-united with his wife. Together they sang Psalm 126:1-3.

When the Lord brought back
   the captivity of Zion,
We were like those who dream.
Then our mouth was filled with laughter,
And our tongue with singing.
Then they said among the nations,
"The Lord has done great things for them."
The Lord has done great things for us,
And we are glad.

ଛଏଓଔ

Chapter 19

From China to the World

After Brother Yun's escape from prison, the Chinese authorities continued to search for him. God made it clear it was time for him and his family to leave China.

But how would they do that? The authorities said Yun was a "dangerous criminal." He could be arrested at the airport.

A Christian friend said, "You can use my passport, Brother Yun. I'm willing to take any trouble that may come on me because of it."

Yun received the passport with thanks. But then he looked at the photo on the passport. How would this passport work? This businessman didn't look anything like him. He was an older man. He was bald. And he wore glasses. Yun was younger. He had plenty of hair and no glasses. What would he do? What would the airport officials think?

But Yun wanted to follow the Lord, and the Lord said "Go." So they bought the ticket.

September 28, 1997 was the day to fly to Germany. The day before he left, Brother Yun spoke at a little Bible school in China's capital city.

"God has told me to take the gospel of Jesus Christ to the west and south," he said. "I used to think He just meant the area around my village. Now I know He was talking about the entire world. My plane leaves tomorrow, and God will make the way clear. Please pray for me. Pray especially from this evening until tomorrow afternoon. That's when the flight leaves."

The Bible school students stayed up all night. They cried out to God with tears for God to protect Brother Yun. Yun also stayed up all night asking

God for protection. He knew if he was arrested he would most likely face death.

The Lord encouraged them with many words of Scripture.

The next morning Yun arrived at the airport. He handed that passport to the airport officer. But the officer looked at the photo and laughed. "This isn't you!" he said. "Hey everybody, come look at this passport photo! This man is trying to use a fake passport!"

Other airport workers came over. They laughed too.

God's peace came down on Brother Yun. He smiled calmly and said nothing.

The officer made Brother Yun wait and wait. Finally the officer spoke to him again. "It's obvious this passport isn't yours. But when you get to Germany, they'll send you back. So go."

Yun boarded that plane for Germany! He arrived safely and was received in Germany too.

God spoke to his heart.

I brought you out of prison. I brought you out of China. In the same mighty way, I will bring thou- of My children out of China. They will be My witnesses all through Asia.

శుంఁ

In time, Yun's family was reunited with him in Germany. Now Yun travels and speaks around the globe. He speaks mighty words of truth and love.

He tells how much the world needs the gospel of Jesus Christ.

He tells how God's children must be willing to suffer for Him, for His gospel to go out against the enemies.

He tells of the importance of praying in faith.

And he tells what great miracles God wants to work, in us and through us, for His glory.

A Message to Parents

Because this biography is written for children, the persecution Brother Yun experienced is described with a minimum of detail. It was extremely intense persecution, however, and he describes it more fully in his own autobiography, *The Heavenly Man,* co-written with Paul Hattaway. In that book, Brother Yun also describes the terrible strain his work put on his family, as well as the ways in which his own selfishness and pride sometimes contributed to his imprisonments.

Biography writers are often castigated nowadays for writing hagiographies unless they take care to show the flaws and sins of their subject. I choose to limit the flaws of any person I write about in my children's biographies, so if that makes me a hagiographer, I apologize. I think of my biographies as simply introductions to the lives of those who have lived as examples for the rest of us.

If this taste of Brother Yun's life has interested you in more, I encourage you to read the whole story in his own book. There you'll see a flawed man who has erred and repented and struggled, but still followed the Lord with great faith. That faith is what is exemplary for us all.

About the Author

Rebecca Davis and her husband, Tim, homeschooled their four children for 25 years, in Indiana, New York, and South Carolina. With their children grown, they now live in Greenville, South Carolina, where their home hosts many guests.

When she was young, Rebecca enjoyed reading biographies. Now she enjoys writing them. Besides the Potter's Wheel series of Christian bio-graphies for children and their families, Rebecca is also the author of the Hidden Heroes series of true missionary stories, also for children and their families. At *www.hiddenheroesmissionarystories.com* you can see all her books for children, her storytelling presentations, and "what people are saying." You can also read a sample chapter of each book and sample devotionals from her devotional books.

You can connect with Rebecca through her website and at *rebecca@hiddenheroesmissionarystories.com.*

Potter's Wheel Books #1
Fanny Crosby
Queen of Gospel Songs

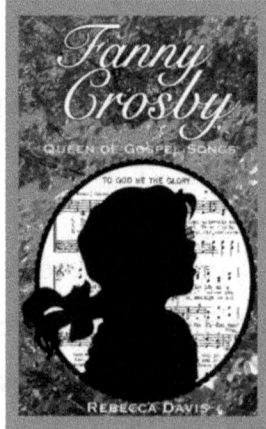

The man said he was a doctor . . . but he did something to little baby Fanny's eyes that made her blind for the rest of her life. How could she find out about the world around her? How could she be happy? How could she learn? How could she love God? How could she forgive?

Fanny Crosby was blind for more than ninety years . . . and she wrote over 8,000 hymns and gospel songs about her Savior.

At *www.hiddenheroesmissionarystories.com* you can read a sample chapter.

Potter's Wheel Books #2
Joy Ridderhof
Voice Catcher Around the World

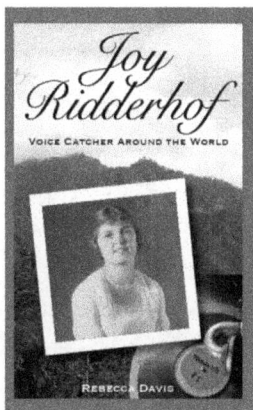

Joy Ridderhof loved being a missionary to Honduras. But when she had to go home very sick, the Lord changed all her plans. She began recording gospel records in Spanish. Then in more languages. And more . . . and more . . . and more.

Joy traveled all over the world, recording the voices of remote tribal people speaking the gospel, and having plenty of adventures along the way. Today the mission work she started has recorded the gospel in over *six thousand languages.* Read more about her at *www.hiddenheroes-missionarystories.com.*

Potter's Wheel Books #3
George Mueller
Pickpocket to Praying Provider

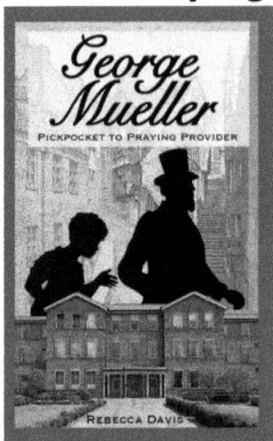

When people weren't looking, *he stole from them.* He stole from his father. He even stole from his pastor.

But one day George Mueller found out that the God he had been pretending to worship was real. Now, instead of taking from others, he wanted to give to help others. By the end of his life, George Mueller had given over a million dollars. But where did he get it?

He asked God. And God gave . . . and gave . . . and gave. George Mueller used the money God gave him to provide homes for over ten thousand orphans. Read a sample chapter at *www.hiddenheroesmissionarystories.com.*

Hidden Heroes #1
With Two Hands:
Stories of God at Work in Ethiopia

Why would a slave and a witch doctor walk for three days to find the white man called Jesus? Why would a crippled old man wait by the side of the road every day for twenty years? Why would a lame man purposely walk to a tribe where he knew he could be killed?

Written on the upper-elementary level, sixteen true missionary stories taken from the ministry of one missionary show the power of God in the midst of darkness, among people of Ethiopia who saw the great light of the gospel. You can visit *www.hiddenheroesmissionarystories.com* to read a sample chapter.

Hidden Heroes #2
The Good News Must Go Out:
Stories of God at Work
in the Central African Republic

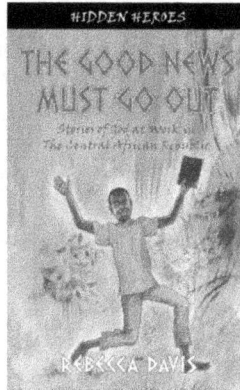

A sultan whose 300 wives were buried alive . . . cannibals who believed there was no such thing as a white woman . . . an elegant French lady who watched in horror as the missionary performed surgery on her kitchen table.

These are just a few of the real people in these true missionary stories of Margaret Laird in her ministry in the Central African Republic, as she and many others gave their lives in service of the King of Glory, whose Good News could not be stopped. To read a sample chapter, visit *www.hiddenheroesmissionarystories.com.*

Hidden Heroes #3
Witness Men: True Stories of God at Work in Papua, Indonesia

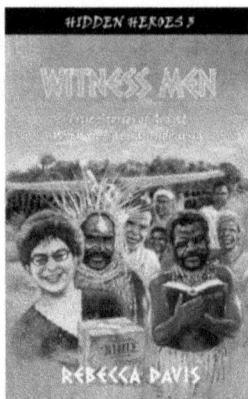

In 1938, in the remote highlands of a mountainous island, explorers discovered thousands upon thousands of tribal people. Missionaries began to come, to bring the Good News of the Gospel, to tell them about Jesus. Little did they know that many of the people of the tribes had been waiting . . . waiting . . . for someone to come and help them out of the darkness of their old way of life.

Fifteen chapters on the upper-elementary level tell the true missionary stories of the gospel spreading throughout the highlands of Papua, Indonesia, from 1955 to 2010, when one of the tribes received their first New Testaments

Hidden Heroes #4
Return of the White Book:
True Stories of God at Work in Southeast Asia

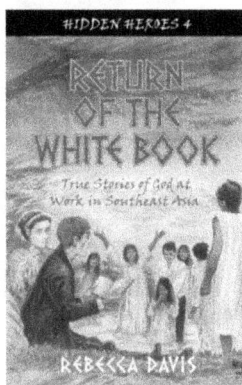

When Adoniram Judson took the Gospel, the good news about the Lord Jesus, to the people of Burma in 1813, he didn't know that high up in the hills lived a tribe of people whose ancient stories and songs served as continual reminders that one day the White Book that their ancestors had lost would be brought back to them.

Sixteen chapters on the upper-elementary level tell stories of the transformation that the Word of God brought to the Hill Tribes of Southeast Asia. To read a sample chapter, visit *www.hiddenheroesmissionarystories.com.*

Hidden Heroes #5
Lights in a Dark Place: True Stories
of God at Work in Colombia

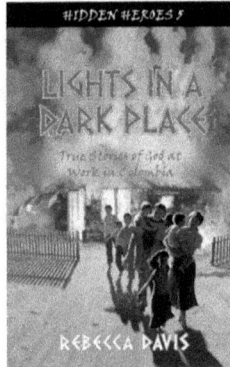

Colombia has been known as a land of violence, but God is at work! Even though the Colombian people have reacted with violence to the gospel of Jesus Christ, God has delivered people from burning houses ... God has given people dreams and visions ... God has rescued kidnapers ... God has conquered demons of darkness.

Read fourteen true stories of the Light of the World shining in the land of Colombia, South America. Published 2014 by Christian Focus Publications. Read a sample chapter at *www.hiddenheroesmissionarystories.com.*

Hidden Heroes #6
Living Water in the Desert:
True Stories of God at Work in Iran

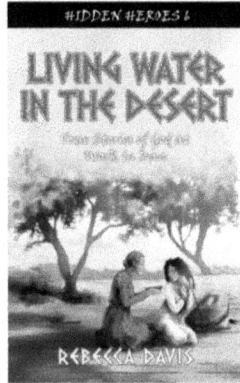

One man was overcome by the missionary's kindness. Another was stopped by a vision of men in blue. One became sick and tired of his own religion. Another saw a man named Jesus in a dream, coming to him on a donkey. A girl found a strange book on the floor of the library and visited a secret prayer meeting.

Seventeen chapters tell true stories of the Living Water pouring out on the country of Iran. And it's still happening! The most recent story in this book took place in 2013. Published by Christian Focus Publications 2015. Visit the website *www.hiddenheroesmissionarystories.com* to read a sample chapter.

101 Devotionals for Girls
from the Lives of Great Christians

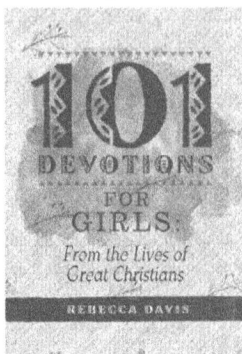

Read 101 short devotionals based on the lives of missionaries and other Christians in the Hidden Heroes and Potter's Wheel books. Meet mighty women of God like Elinor Young, Mary Bird, and Margaret Nicholl Laird. Some of these women's names aren't well known, but they should be!

Each devotional begins with a story and ends with a challenge. Each one contains a Scripture and a prayer. They're ideally suited for young people in middle school and high school.

Visit *www.hiddenheroesmissionarystories.com* to read a few sample devotionals.

101 Devotionals for Guys from the Lives of Great Christians

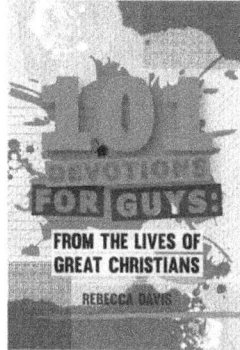

Read 101 short devotionals based on the lives of missionaries and other Christians in the Hidden Heroes and Potter's Wheel books. Meet mighty men of God like Russell Stendal, George Boardman, and Dick McLellan. Some of these men's names aren't well known, but they should be!

Each devotional begins with a story and ends with a challenge. Each one contains a Scripture and a prayer. They're ideal for young people in middle school and high school.

Visit *www.hiddenheroesmissionarystories.com* to read a few sample devotionals.

www.ingramcontent.com/pod-product-compliance
Lightning Source LLC
Chambersburg PA
CBHW071600040426

42452CB00008B/1246